Getting

to know

yourself

Journal

A journal with prompts to have fun learning
about yourself in your everyday life

This book was made because some days are just no
Fun and we need a way to have more fun.
Journaling can help get your feelings out, but now
you can learn a little about yourself at the same time.

Tamara L Adams

Tammy@tamaraladamsauthor.com

tamaraadamsauthor@gmail.com

www.tamaraladamsauthor.com

https://twitter.com/@TamaraLAdams

https://www.facebook.com/TamaraLAdamsAuthor/

http://www.amazon.com/T.L.-Adams/e/B00YSROGC4

https://www.pinterest.com/Tjandlexismom/tamara-l-adams-author/

Table of Contents

38. What is your favorite board game and why
39. What would you do if locked in a Wal-Mart all night
40. Describe your favorite pet you have/want
41. What have you always wanted to learn
42. What would you put on pizza all at once and why
43. What is your best personality trait
44. Write something positive on the page (anything)
45. Describe your dream home
46. What is your favorite amusement park ride/memory
47. Write about your favorite piece of jewelry
48. What will you do tomorrow to make it a better day
49. What decade would you travel to and why
50. Describe your favorite sport
51. Make me crave your favorite dessert
52. Describe a magical world you know of or make up
53. Where would you choose to retire and why
54. What kind of tattoo would you get
55. What would you do if you were the last person alive
56. If you could be an animal what would you choose
57. Write about your favorite book
58. Make me want to eat at your favorite restaurant
59. Describe your favorite outfit
60. What extinct animal would you bring back alive
61. Write about a day spent with your favorite person
62. Describe y our favorite holiday
63. Write the same word over and over again
64. What is your mood right now and why
65. What dangerous activity would you like to do
66. Describe the best concert you have ever seen
67. What is your favorite sport to watch and why
68. Plan the perfect weekend getaway
69. What would you write a TV show about
70. Write all y our brilliant ideas on this page
71. What is your favorite memory and why
72. Change the ending of your least favorite day
73. What change do you want to see in the world
74. What would you put into a time capsule
75. What happened today that made you happy

76. What actor would play you in your life's movie
77. Write what type of ice cream flavor you would make
78. Turn all your negative thoughts into good ones here
79. Change the ending of a book you read
80. What can you teach the world
81. What have you accomplished in life
82. List five goals for your life and how you will attain them
83. What do you have to confess
84. Dear future self
85. Describe the perfect flower
86. Write all y our worries on this page
87. What is your desire
88. Describe the funniest time you ever had
89. Who is your celebrity crush and why
90. What is your greatest fear and how will you overcome it
91. Describe your favorite teacher
92. Who always believes in you
93. What would be your three wishes
94. Where do you want to be in five years
95. Who is your hero and why
96. What is your favorite weather and why
97. When were you brave
98. List five places you would like to visit and why
99. Do you think there are aliens (why or why not)
100.   Finish the story: There once was a boy/girl who

Find a prompt that suits your mood and write on!

1. What is your favorite childhood memory

_____
_____
_____
_____
_____
_____
_____
_____
_____
_____
_____
_____
_____
_____
_____
_____
_____
_____
_____
_____
_____
_____
_____
_____
_____
_____
_____
_____
_____
_____

2. Name the best quality of your significant other/friend

3. What advice would you give your younger self

4. What song makes you want to dance and why

5. What is your one wish for the world

6. What would your superpower be

7. What is your best quality

8. If you could travel to one place where you go

_____
_____
_____
_____
_____
_____
_____
_____
_____
_____
_____
_____
_____
_____
_____
_____
_____
_____
_____
_____
_____
_____
_____
_____
_____
_____
_____

9. What would you write a book about

10. Describe your most positively influential person

11. What is your favorite movie and why

_____

_____

_____

_____

_____

_____

_____

_____

_____

_____

_____

_____

_____

_____

_____

_____

_____

_____

_____

_____

_____

_____

_____

_____

_____

12. Write a love letter to your love or future love

13. Describe your dream job

14. Where/why would you volunteer if you had the time

_____

_____

_____

_____

_____

_____

_____

_____

_____

_____

_____

_____

_____

_____

_____

_____

_____

_____

_____

_____

_____

_____

_____

_____

_____

_____

15. Write about your passion

16. What is your one wish for yourself

17. Describe the best day of your life so far

_____

_____

_____

_____

_____

_____

_____

_____

_____

_____

_____

_____

_____

_____

_____

_____

_____

_____

_____

_____

_____

_____

_____

_____

_____

18. Write a bucket list of 25 things you wish you go do

19. List one of your flaws and how you will improve

20. Describe the perfect vacation

21. What non-profit organization would you start

22. What is your favorite physical asset

23. How would you inspire someone feeling down

24. If you were president, what would you do

_____

_____

_____

_____

_____

_____

_____

_____

_____

_____

_____

_____

_____

_____

_____

_____

_____

_____

_____

_____

_____

_____

_____

_____

_____

_____

_____

_____

25. Write something nice on this page for a stranger

26. Make a boring event sound better than it was

27. Write down your favorite quotes or sayings

_____

_____
_____
_____
_____
_____
_____
_____
_____
_____
_____
_____
_____
_____
_____
_____
_____
_____
_____
_____
_____
_____
_____
_____
_____
_____
_____

28. Describe a fun day or date using no money

29. Write what annoys you on this page

30. Write all your favorite thoughts on this page

31. Write a happy place dream monologue

32. What would you would do if you won a million

_____

_____

_____

_____

_____

_____

_____

_____

_____

_____

_____

_____

_____

_____

_____

_____

_____

_____

_____

_____

_____

_____

_____

_____

_____

33. Dear Past Self

34. If you could own your own business what would it be

35. Describe your favorite person/people

36. What Olympic event would you want to compete in

37. Who inspires you the most and why

38. What is your favorite board game and why

39. What would you do if locked in a Wal-Mart all

40. Describe your favorite pet you have/want

_____

_____

_____

_____

_____

_____

_____

_____

_____

_____

_____

_____

_____

_____

_____

_____

_____

_____

_____

_____

_____

_____

_____

_____

_____

_____

_____

_____

_____

_____

41. What have you always wanted to learn

42. What would you put on pizza all at once and why

43. What is your best personality trait

_____

_____

_____

_____

_____

_____

_____

_____

_____

_____

_____

_____

_____

_____

_____

_____

_____

_____

_____

_____

_____

_____

_____

_____

_____

_____

_____

44. Write something positive on the page (anything)

45. Describe your dream home

_____

_____

_____

_____

_____

_____

_____

_____

_____

_____

_____

_____

_____

_____

_____

_____

_____

_____

_____

_____

_____

_____

_____

_____

_____

_____

46. What is your favorite amusement park ride/memory

47. Write about your favorite piece of jewelry

48. What will you do tomorrow to make it a better

49. What decade would you travel to and why

50. Describe your favorite sport

51. Make me crave your favorite dessert

52. Describe a magical world you know of or make up

53. Where would you choose to retire and why

54. What kind of tattoo would you get

55. What would you do if you were the last person

55. If you could be an animal what would you choose

_____

_____

_____

_____

_____

_____

_____

_____

_____

_____

_____

_____

_____

_____

_____

_____

_____

_____

_____

_____

_____

_____

_____

_____

_____

_____

_____

_____

_____

57. Write about your favorite book

58. Make me want to eat at your favorite restaurant

59. Describe your favorite outfit

60. What extinct animal would you bring back alive

61. Write about a day spent with your favorite

_____

_____

_____

_____

_____

_____

_____

_____

_____

_____

_____

_____

_____

_____

_____

_____

_____

_____

_____

_____

_____

_____

_____

_____

_____

62. Describe your favorite holiday

63. Write the same word over and over again

64. What is your mood right now and why

_____

_____

_____

_____

_____

_____

_____

_____

_____

_____

_____

_____

_____

_____

_____

_____

_____

_____

_____

_____

_____

_____

_____

_____

_____

_____

_____

_____

65. What dangerous activity would you like to do

66. Describe the best concert you have ever seen

_____
_____
_____
_____
_____
_____
_____
_____
_____
_____
_____
_____
_____
_____
_____
_____
_____
_____
_____
_____
_____
_____
_____
_____
_____
_____
_____
_____

67. What is your favorite sport to watch and why

68. Plan the perfect weekend getaway

69. What would you write a TV show about

70. Write all y our brilliant ideas on this page

71. What is your favorite memory and why

72. Change the ending of your least favorite day

73. What change do you want to see in the world

74. What would you put into a time capsule

75. What happened today that made you happy

76. What actor would play you in your life's movie

77. Write what type of ice cream flavor you would

_____

_____

_____

_____

_____

_____

_____

_____

_____

_____

_____

_____

_____

_____

_____

_____

_____

_____

_____

_____

_____

_____

_____

_____

78. Turn all your negative thoughts into good ones here

79. Change the ending of a book you read

80. What can you teach the world

81. What have you accomplished in life

82. List 5 goals for your life and how you will attain them

_____

_____

_____

_____

_____

_____

_____

_____

_____

_____

_____

_____

_____

_____

_____

_____

_____

_____

_____

_____

_____

_____

_____

_____

_____

_____

83. What do you have to confess

_____

_____

_____

_____

_____

_____

_____

_____

_____

_____

_____

_____

_____

_____

_____

_____

_____

_____

_____

_____

_____

_____

_____

_____

_____

_____

_____

_____

_____

_____

84. Dear future self

85. Describe the perfect flower

86. Write all y our worries on this page

87. What is your desire

_____
_____
_____
_____
_____
_____
_____
_____
_____
_____
_____
_____
_____
_____
_____
_____
_____
_____
_____
_____
_____
_____
_____
_____
_____
_____

88. Describe the funniest time you ever had

_____

_____

_____

_____

_____

_____

_____

_____

_____

_____

_____

_____

_____

_____

_____

_____

_____

_____

_____

_____

_____

_____

_____

_____

_____

_____

_____

_____

_____

89. Who is your celebrity crush and why

_____
_____
_____
_____
_____
_____
_____
_____
_____
_____
_____
_____
_____
_____
_____
_____
_____
_____
_____
_____
_____
_____
_____
_____
_____
_____
_____
_____

90. Name your greatest fear and how will you overcome it

91. Describe your favorite teacher

92. Who always believes in you

93. What would be your three wishes

94. Where do you want to be in five years

95. Who is your hero and why

96. What is your favorite weather and why

97. When were you brave

98. List five places you would like to visit and why

_____

_____

_____

_____

_____

_____

_____

_____

_____

_____

_____

_____

_____

_____

_____

_____

_____

_____

_____

_____

_____

_____

_____

_____

_____

_____

_____

99. Do you think there are aliens (why or why not)

_____

_____

_____

_____

_____

_____

_____

_____

_____

_____

_____

_____

_____

_____

_____

_____

_____

_____

_____

_____

_____

_____

_____

_____

_____

_____

_____

100. Finish the story: There once was a boy/girl who

_____

_____

_____

_____

_____

_____

_____

_____

_____

_____

_____

_____

_____

_____

_____

_____

_____

_____

_____

_____

_____

_____

_____

_____

_____

_____

_____

_____

Made in the USA
Thornton, CO
02/07/24 16:12:17